Published by Evans Brothers Limited
2A Portman Mansions
Chiltern Street
London W1U 6NR

© Evans Brothers Limited 2004

First published 2004

Printed in China

British Library Cataloguing in Publication data.

Powell, Jillian
Down syndrome. - (Like Me, Like You)
1. Down syndrome - Juvenile literature 2. Developmentally
disabled - Juvenile literature
I. Title
618.9'2858842

ISBN 0237526719

Acknowledgements

The author and publishers would like to thank the following
for their help with this book:

Nicky, Terry and Luke Parker, Paul Thomas and Jenny Roe
and Space Adventure, Swindon.

Thanks also to the UK Down's Syndrome Association for
their help in the preparation of this book.

All photographs by Gareth Boden

Credits

Series Editor: Louise John
Editor: Julia Bird
Designer: Mark Holt
Production: Jenny Mulvanny

HELP FOR PEOPLE WITH DOWN'S SYNDROME
DOWN'S SYNDROME ASSOCIATION
A Registered Charity

LIKE ME LIKE YOU

Luke has
DOWN'S
SYNDROME

JILLIAN POWELL

Evans

Hi, my name is Luke. I live at home with my mum and dad and my brothers, Kenny and Zac. We've got a dog called Dana, six goldfish and three guinea pigs! I like playing football and tennis and going to the cinema.

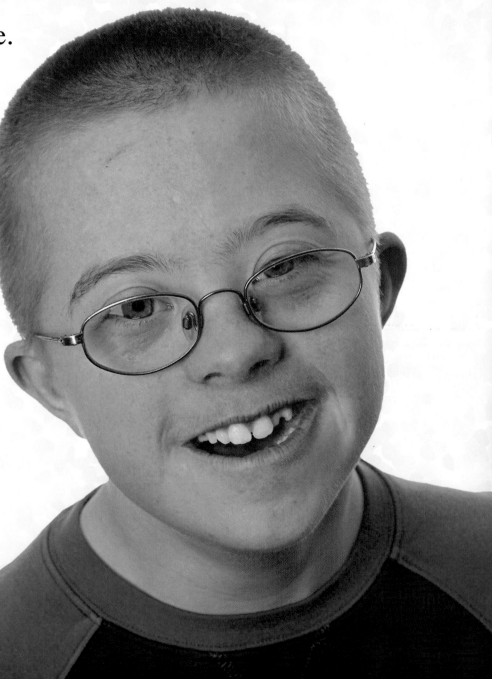

I was born with **Down's syndrome.** It means I look a bit different from most people and I have some **learning difficulties**.

DOWN'S SYNDROME

About one in a thousand babies is born with Down's syndrome.

Having Down's syndrome means I sometimes need extra help with things. I like to help too, though. Today I set the table for breakfast, then I help Mum eat up the sausages!

I need extra help learning words. Mum helps me at home and I have special lessons to help me talk and read at school too. I have to pick a letter on the cards that matches the picture Mum shows me.

EXTRA HELP

Children with Down's syndrome need extra help learning to talk and read.

Today, we're going to the
adventure playground.
I'm ringing my
friend Paul to
see if he can
come too.
I dial Paul's
number. Mum
has written it
down for me.

Paul lives on my road and we go to cub scouts together every week. We're going to pick him up on the way to the playground.

GLUE EAR

Like many children with Down's syndrome, Luke sometimes has **glue ear** which makes it difficult for him to hear. He often wears hearing aids to help him hear better.

Mum and I walk to Paul's house to meet him. When I go out, I need help to look out for traffic and cross the road safely.

We're catching the bus to the adventure playground. Someone has to tell me when to put out my hand to stop the right bus!

There are lots of things to do at the adventure playground.
Paul and I love going on the giant slides!

It's time for a break. We buy a drink and a snack at the restaurant. Paul helps me count out the money to pay.

Now we're trying out the ball pool! Paul and I practise throwing and catching the balls between us.

This is a kind of see-saw. We try bouncing up and down on it. It's great fun but I keep falling off!

Every child with Down's syndrome is different. Some have more learning difficulties than others. Others have health problems to do with their ears, chest or heart.

On the way home, Paul tells me it's his mum's birthday. We stop at the flower shop so we can buy her some flowers. I use **Makaton signing** to help me explain which flowers I want.

I like red flowers best, so I sign the colour red. The lady helps us choose a lovely bunch of flowers.

MAKATON SIGNING

Some children with Down's syndrome learn Makaton signing before they can talk. They use it to help others understand them.

Paul and I go to cub scouts in the church hall once a week. I get dressed in my cub's uniform. Sometimes I need a bit of help getting dressed. Dad helps me tie my scarf.

Every week, we start by raising the flag. Then the cub leader tells us what we're going to do today. Dad stands behind me to help. He says everything again, and speaks slowly and clearly so I can understand what I need to do.

Today we're playing one of my favourite games. It's called the ball and bottle game. We get into two teams. We're each given a number and when your number is called out you have to run to the chair.

You have to try to knock the bottle over before the cub from the other team does. The first one to knock the bottle over wins a point for his team.

We do crafts too. Today we've made puppets from The Jungle Book. I watch the other cubs to help me understand what to do. We put on a play with the puppets for the other cubs.

The cub leader usually gives out badges before we go home. I've got badges for swimming, art, first aid and lots of other things.

When I get home, I watch television with my brother Zac. Dad usually reads to me before I go to sleep. I can only read a few words myself but I like listening to stories, especially adventure stories.

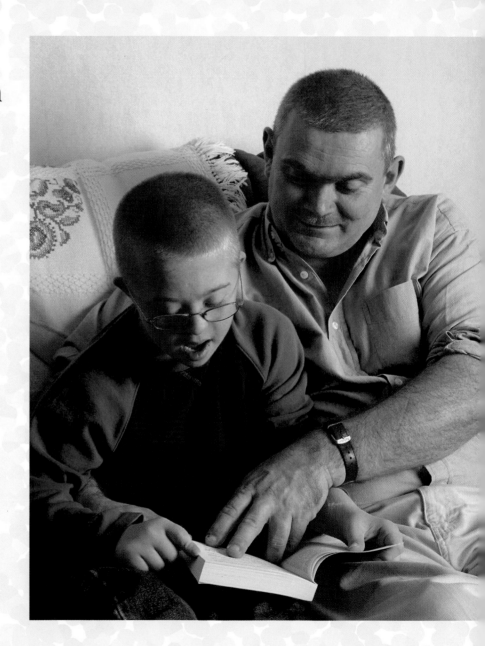

Having Down's syndrome means I need extra help with some things at home and at school. But there are lots of things I can do that I enjoy, like football and cubs, and taking my dog Dana for walks!

Glossary

Down's syndrome babies born with Down's syndrome have a slightly different cell make-up from most people. It affects the way they look and also gives them some learning difficulties

Glue ear a condition in which sticky fluid builds up in the ear. It can cause hearing loss, particularly in children

Learning difficulties when someone needs extra help to learn reading and writing and other skills

Makaton signing a way of making signs with the hands to help someone understand what you are saying

Index

Further Information

UNITED KINGDOM
UK Down's Syndrome Association
Tel: 020 8682 4001
www.downs-syndrome.org.uk
Provides information and support for people with Down's syndrome, their families, carers and those with a professional interest.

UNITED STATES OF AMERICA
National Association for Down's Syndrome
Tel: 630 325 9112
www.nads.org
Information, facts and family stories.

AUSTRALIA
ACT Down's Syndrome Association
Tel: (02) 6290 0656
www.actdsa.asn.au
Provides support and information to families and aims to improve quality of life for those with Down's syndrome.

NEW ZEALAND
Downs Syndrome Association of New Zealand
Tel: 09 307 7945
www.nas.com/downsyn/newzea.html
Support group for families caring for children and adults with Down's syndrome.

www.makaton.org
A website explaining the language of Makaton signing.

BOOKS
Friends at the Seaside,
Diane Church, Franklin Watts 2000

What Does It Mean to Have Down's Syndrome?
Louise Spilsbury, Heinemann Library, 2002

We'll Paint the Octopus Red,
Stephanie Stuve Bodeen, Woodbine House 1998

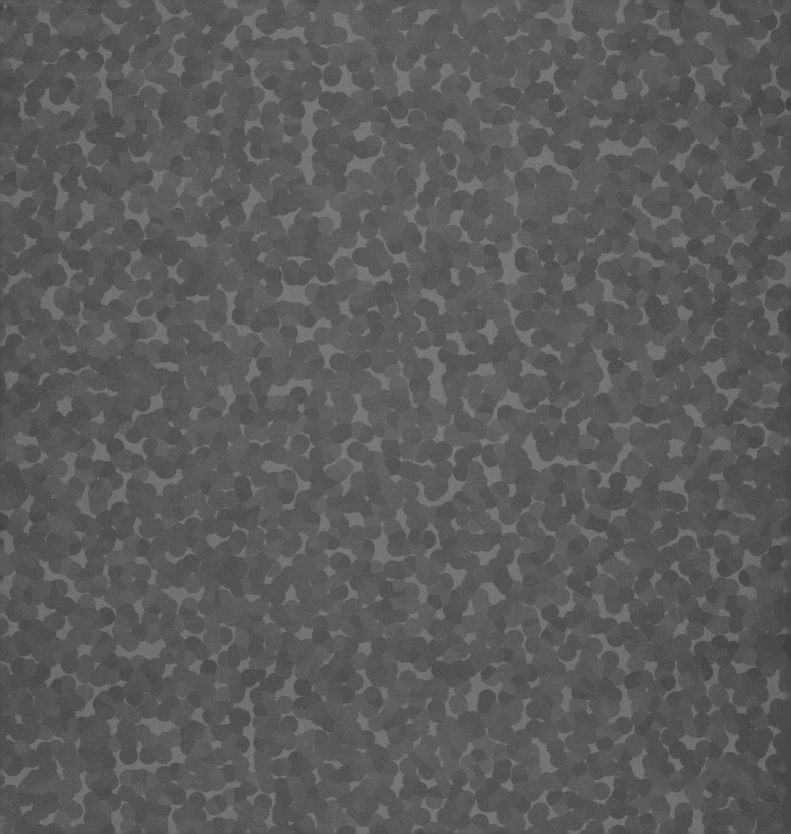